20th Century Inventions

NUCLEAR POWER

Nina Morgan

WAYLAND

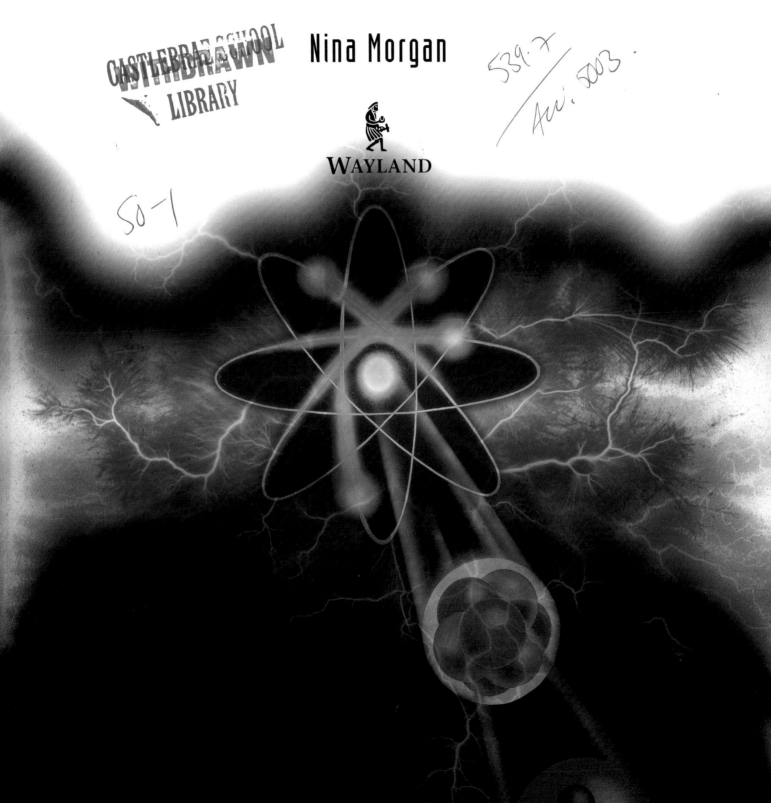

20th Century Inventions

AIRCRAFT

CARS

COMPUTERS

THE INTERNET

LASERS

NUCLEAR POWER

ROCKETS AND SPACECRAFT

SATELLITES

TELECOMMUNICATIONS

Front cover and title page: Diagram of the structure of the atom.
Back cover: Sellafield nuclear power and reprocessing plant, Cumbria, UK.

Series editor: Philippa Smith
Book editor: Liz Harman
Series designer: Tim Mayer
Book designer: Malcolm Walker of Kudos Design
Cover designer: Dennis Day

First published in 1997 by Wayland Publishers Limited,
61 Western Road, Hove, East Sussex BN3 1JD, England

Find Wayland on the internet at http://www.wayland.co.uk

British Library Cataloguing in Publication Data
Morgan, Nina
  Nuclear power. – (Twentieth century inventions)
  1. Nuclear energy – Juvenile literature 2. Nuclear power
  plants – Juvenile literature
  I. Title
  539.7

ISBN 0 7502 2034 1

Typeset by Malcolm Walker
Printed and bound in Italy by G. Canale & C.S.p.A., Turin

Picture acknowledgements
BNFL (British Nuclear Fuels Plc) 11, 17 (bottom), 20, 21 (right) 26 (both); Hulton Getty 6 (bottom) and 44 (top), 29; New Zealand High Commission 41; Science Photo Library front cover (composite) Michael Gilbert/Henry Dakin/Phil Jude, back cover Jeremy Burgess, 6 (top)/Argonne National Laboratory 9 (top)/Bill Bachmann 15/Alex Bartel 16, 19/Arthus Bertrand 13 (bottom)/Martin Bond 4, 18 (bottom)/Simon Fraser 40/Koschemsahr 22/Bsip Leca 34/Los Alamos National Laboratory 8, 9 (bottom)/Jerry Mason 43 and 45 (bottom)/Mere Words 21 (left)/Hank Morgan 37/Larry Mulvehill 36/Novosti 23 and 45 (middle)/Catherine Pouedras 17 (top)/Roger Ressmeyer, Starlight 18 (top), 24/US Department of Energy 12, 25, 27, 35, 42; Topham Picturepoint 7 and 44 (bottom), 28 and 44 (middle), 33 (bottom), 38, 39; TRH 32; Wayland Picture Library 14; Zefa Picture Library contents and 30, 5, 13 (top). Artwork by Tim Benké, Top Draw, (Tableaux).

20th Century Inventions
CONTENTS

UNLIMITED POWER FOR ALL?

We all use energy – lots of it! Almost everything you can think of, from heating and lighting, running communications and computer systems to cleaning our water, involves the use of energy. The world's demand for energy is increasing. The World Energy Council estimates that by the year 2020 the world will be using 50 per cent more energy than we do today.

Energy to burn

Energy is produced in a number of ways. It can be obtained by burning fossil fuels such as coal, oil and gas, or biomass fuels such as wood, crop wastes or animal dung. Energy can be captured from renewable sources – sources that will never run out – such as the Sun and the natural forces of waves, tides and the wind, or from heat below the Earth's surface.

But one of the most plentiful sources of energy – the atom – is all around us. All matter is made of atoms. Each minute atom contains large amounts of energy in its nucleus, or core. This nuclear energy can be released and used.

The awesome power of nuclear energy first became clear to the world during the Second World War (1939–45), when the first atomic bombs were dropped on Japan. The death and destruction that they caused horrified people all over the world.

Nuclear power from reactors like the Sellafield nuclear plant in Cumbria, UK, produces around 17 per cent of the world's electricity. In some countries, such as France, nuclear power is the main source of electricity.

Power for the future

But people could also see that nuclear power promised to be a cheap, plentiful and relatively pollution-free energy for all sorts of uses. In the 1950s and '60s, some people even predicted that nuclear energy could produce unlimited supplies of electricity so cheaply that power companies might even supply it to their customers free of charge.

This has not come true. Nuclear power plants produce just 17 per cent of the world's electricity and the electricity they produce is not as inexpensive as people once imagined it would be.

Problems to solve

The nuclear industry has one big problem to solve – safety. Nuclear power plants use a radioactive fuel and produce radioactive waste. No one has yet found the perfect way to dispose of the waste safely or to ensure that radioactivity never leaks from a nuclear reactor, even during an accident.

Many people are so worried about the safety of nuclear power that they want to ban nuclear power plants. In Sweden, where nuclear power provides half of the country's energy needs, people have voted to get rid of their nuclear power plants and look for other ways of producing electricity.

The ruins of the Japanese city of Hiroshima after the first atomic bomb used in war was dropped on 6 August 1945.

Where does the world's energy come from?

The world currently obtains its energy from the following sources:

oil:	37.9%
gas:	20%
coal:	30%
nuclear power:	5.3%
hydroelectric power:	6.8%.

France, the world's main user of nuclear power, obtains 72.9% of its total electricity from nuclear power.

5

THE POWER OF THE ATOM

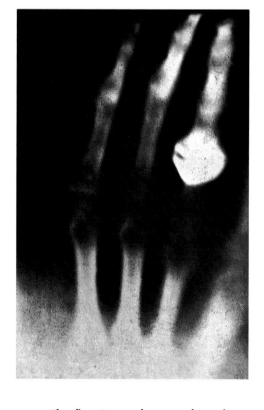

The he development of nuclear power really began in 1895 with an X-ray of a woman's hand. The picture was made by the German scientist Wilhelm Röntgen, and the hand belonged to his wife. While carrying out experiments using electricity and light, Röntgen noticed some unusual rays that seemed to penetrate where light could not. He named them X-rays. Many people were very excited by his discovery. Soon, other scientists began to notice unusual rays too.

The first X-ray photograph, a view of his wife's hand wearing a ring, taken by Wilhelm Röntgen in 1895.

A year later, the French scientist Henri Becquerel noticed that the chemical element uranium gave off different rays, or radiation, that blackened a photographic plate. Becquerel had discovered radioactivity – the tendency for atoms of some elements to decay, or break down, giving off energy and atomic particles.

A few years later, French scientists Pierre and Marie Curie found two other radioactive elements, polonium and radium. More were discovered later and we now know of nine naturally occurring radioactive elements.

Understanding the atom

Scientists wanted to know what caused radioactivity and whether its power could be harnessed for useful purposes. Finding answers to these questions took a long time.

Wilhelm Röntgen, the German scientist who discovered X-rays. Röntgen was awarded the Nobel Prize in 1901 for his scientific work.

The first clues began to appear when the British scientists, Joseph John Thompson, Ernest Rutherford and James Chadwick, showed that atoms are not solid objects, but instead have a centre, or nucleus, that has a positive electrical charge and is surrounded by outer layers made up of particles that have a negative electrical charge.

Another clue was found in 1919 when Rutherford bombarded nitrogen atoms with streams of particles. To everyone's amazement, the nitrogen atoms were changed into oxygen. Although nobody yet understood how this happened, Rutherford had caused the atoms to undergo a process called fission and they had split apart. This reaction is used today in nuclear reactors to release energy from atoms.

Enrico Fermi, one of the scientists whose research led to the discovery of how to harness the power of nuclear fission. Fermi's work was recognized in 1938 when he won the Nobel Prize for physics.

Harnessing fission

In 1934, the Italian scientist Enrico Fermi discovered some important clues about how to harness fission when he bombarded atoms with neutrons and found that the amount of radioactive material that was produced depended on the speed at which the neutrons were travelling.

Fermi also discovered that when uranium was bombarded with neutrons, it split into two lighter fragments and gave off energy along with two or three extra neutrons. This suggested that once the fission reaction was started up, the neutrons given off when one uranium atom was split could, in turn, hit other uranium atoms and cause them to break up, releasing yet more neutrons in a chain reaction.

Useful power

Enrico Fermi's work offered important clues about how the fission reaction could be controlled to provide a useful source of power. Many scientists were excited at the prospect of using these discoveries to find out more about the atom. But, before research started, the Second World War broke out. The British and US Governments knew that German scientists had also carried out fission experiments. They were worried that the Germans would use their knowledge about nuclear fission to build a bomb because, if it is not controlled, the fission chain reaction can cause huge explosions.

Britain and the USA set up atomic bomb projects of their own. The most important was a US-led project code-named Manhattan. Many famous scientists worked on the scheme and, in 1945, their work resulted in the building of the first atomic bombs.

Three of the engineers who worked on the Manhattan Project: (from left to right) E.O. Lawrence, Enrico Fermi and I.I. Rabi.

The first nuclear reactor

On 2 December 1942, the first controlled self-sustaining nuclear reaction took place in a squash court at the University of Chicago, USA.

The reactor was very simple. It was made of a pile of blocks of graphite, a crystalline form of carbon, with rods of uranium in between them. The success of the experiment proved that it would be possible to use a controlled nuclear chain reaction to make a powerful bomb.

The experiment was carried out by a team led by Enrico Fermi as part of the Manhattan Project. The team sent a dramatic coded message to the project organizers: 'The Italian navigator has just landed in the New World'. Just three years later, the first atomic bomb was completed.

A layer in the atomic pile that was used to create the first self-sustaining nuclear chain reaction, on 2 December 1942.

The explosion of the first atomic bomb during secret tests carried out at Los Alamos, USA on 16 July 1945 as part of the Manhattan Project. Less than one month later, an atomic bomb destroyed the Japanese city of Hiroshima.

Peaceful uses for nuclear power

After the war, scientists began to concentrate on developing nuclear energy for peaceful purposes. The world's first nuclear power station, Calder Hall in the UK, began generating electricity in 1956. Now there are nuclear power plants in 29 countries around the world. Nuclear power has found many other uses, in medicine, scientific research and as a power source for submarines and spacecraft.

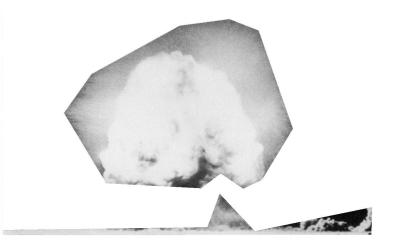

ENERGY FROM ATOMS

It takes energy to hold the particles of an atom together. It is possible to release some of this energy by splitting them apart, in a process known as fission, or forcing them to join up together, in a process called fusion.

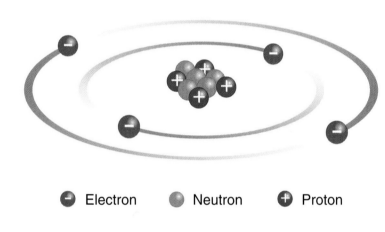

Electron   Neutron   Proton

The structure of the atom.

The structure of atoms

Atoms are made up of three main particles: protons, which carry a positive electrical charge; electrons, which have a negative electrical charge; and neutrons, which are neutral (have no electrical charge).

The centre of the atom, the nucleus, is made up of neutrons and protons. The electrons move around the nucleus in a series of shells. The electrons are held in place because they are attracted to the positive charge in the nucleus.

What are isotopes?

The nature of an atom is determined by the number of protons that it has. All atoms of the same chemical element will have the same number of protons in their nuclei. But they may not have the same number of neutrons.

Atoms of the same element that have different numbers of neutrons in their nuclei are called isotopes. Most elements have several isotopes.

Radioactivity

Many naturally occurring isotopes are stable, which means that their nuclei remain the same. In others, the nucleus is unstable.

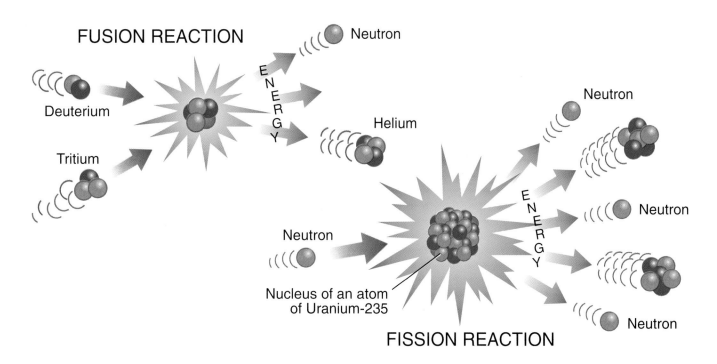

FUSION REACTION

Deuterium

Tritium

Neutron

ENERGY

Helium

Neutron

Nucleus of an atom
of Uranium-235

FISSION REACTION

ENERGY

Neutron

Neutron

Neutron

This means that it changes and breaks apart until it becomes more stable. As it disintegrates it radiates (gives off) energy and atomic particles. These isotopes are described as being radioactive.

Uranium and radium are among the most familiar natural radioactive elements, but there are many others.

Fission

When an atom is hit by a stray neutron its nucleus can split into two parts and release energy and neutrons. This process of splitting atoms is called fission. The neutrons released by fission, in turn, hit other atoms to cause them to split. As more and more atoms break up, more neutrons are released to hit other atoms in a chain reaction.

Fusion

Another way of releasing energy from atoms is by forcing them to fuse, or join together. It is possible to cause fusion to take place on Earth, but it is not easy. Scientists have not yet found a good way of using fusion to generate power, but they are working on it (see pages 42–43).

The processes of nuclear fusion and nuclear fission. Both fission and fusion release energy from atoms.

A uranium mine. Uranium ore is mined in various parts of the world, including the USA, Canada and Australia.

Releasing atomic energy

During the process of fission, large amounts of energy and heat are released. The nuclear power plants operating today use the energy and heat released by the fission of uranium atoms to produce steam. The steam drives a turbine which generates electricity.

Nuclear fuel

The most common fuel used for generating nuclear power in a fission reactor is uranium-235. This isotope is chosen because it splits more easily than other uranium isotopes when it is hit by a neutron.

A researcher loading a nuclear fuel rod with pellets of uranium oxide. He is protected from radiation by a special screen and handles the rod wearing protective gloves.

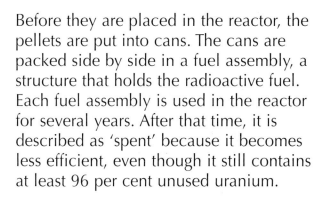

Natural uranium contains only 0.7 per cent uranium-235. Before it is used in reactors, the uranium is enriched (made more concentrated) to raise the level of uranium-235 to 2–3 per cent.

Nuclear fuel rods.

To make fuel for reactors, a combination of enriched uranium and oxygen is formed into fuel pellets. These are packed with energy. Just two pellets could supply enough electricity to last one person for a year. In some types of reactors, one tonne of uranium could produce as much energy as more than a million tonnes of coal.

Before they are placed in the reactor, the pellets are put into cans. The cans are packed side by side in a fuel assembly, a structure that holds the radioactive fuel. Each fuel assembly is used in the reactor for several years. After that time, it is described as 'spent' because it becomes less efficient, even though it still contains at least 96 per cent unused uranium.

In countries such as Britain, France, Germany and Japan, the spent fuel is reprocessed, or treated, so that it can be recycled (used again). Other countries like Sweden and the USA prefer to store spent fuel for future use, or to dispose of it safely as waste.

Fuel rods being removed from the core of a nuclear reactor. The rods are placed in cooling ponds to allow the heat and radiation to die down.

Radiation all around us

Radiation comes in several forms. The most important are alpha and beta particles, X-rays and gamma-rays.

Types of radiation

Alpha and beta radiation are made up of streams of tiny particles travelling at high speed. Alpha radiation is made up of streams of helium nuclei, each containing one neutron and one proton. This form of radiation is slow and heavy. It is easily stopped and cannot pass through paper or skin. It can be harmful if swallowed, or if it enters the body through a break in the skin.

Everyone is exposed to harmless levels of radiation every day, from natural sources as well as from machines like television sets. In such small doses, radiation is not dangerous.

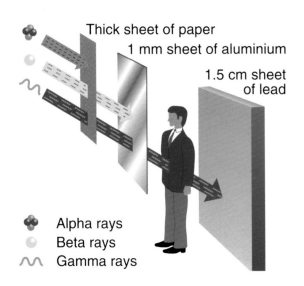

Thick sheet of paper
1 mm sheet of aluminium
1.5 cm sheet
of lead

Alpha rays
Beta rays
Gamma rays

Types of radiation.

In contrast, beta radiation is made up of streams of electrons travelling at high speed. These are lighter and faster than alpha particles. They are also more penetrating, but they can be stopped by a sheet of metal.

X-rays and gamma-rays are pure energy, like light, only far more energetic. These rays are very penetrating. The most energetic forms of gamma-rays can be stopped only by thick layers of lead, steel or concrete.

Radiation in everyday life

Everyone is exposed to some radiation from natural sources such as air, rocks and the Sun, as well as from machines such as televisions and photocopiers and in our food and drink. In addition, we receive small doses of radiation during X-ray examinations, and some radiation escapes from nuclear power stations.

In small doses, radiation is not dangerous. But it must be used very carefully. Large amounts cause chemical changes which can change the way living cells grow, function or reproduce.

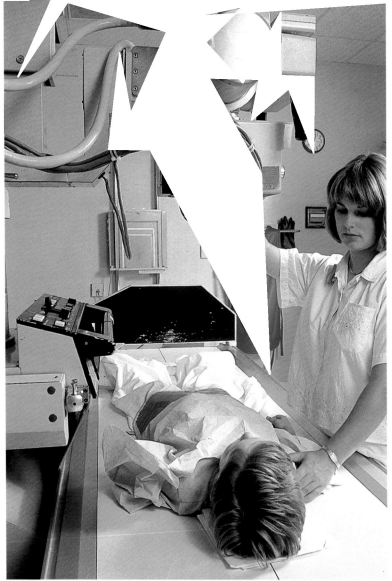

A boy undergoing an X-ray examination. Body tissues absorb X-rays differently. Bones, which are dense, absorb X-rays well and appear white on film. Less absorbent body tissues appear dark.

Half-lives

As radioactive materials decay (break down), their radioactivity reduces. Each material has a half-life. This is the time it takes for the material to decay so that it has half its previous radioactivity. The half-lives of different materials can vary from milliseconds (thousandths of a second) to billions of years.

NUCLEAR REACTORS AND POWER PLANTS

Nuclear power plants work very much like coal-fired power plants. In both types of plant, heat is used to boil water to create high-pressure steam. The steam is used to drive a turbine, a machine in which a fluid is used to push rotor blades around. The turbine generates electricity.

The main difference between them is the source of the heat. In coal-fired plants, heat is produced by burning coal. In nuclear power plants, the heat results from the fission of uranium atoms in a nuclear reactor.

Inside a reactor

Inside the central area of a nuclear reactor, which is called the core, cans containing rods of uranium fuel are laid out in a special way to make up fuel elements. This helps to make sure that enough neutrons will be captured by the uranium to set up a fission chain reaction. The chain reaction is very carefully controlled to ensure that it gives off a constant supply of heat.

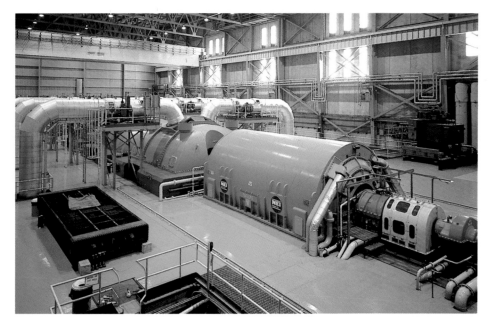

A turbine and electricity generator at the Le Preau nuclear power station in Canada.

To keep the chain reaction going steadily, each fuel element is surrounded by a moderator. The moderator is a material such as water or graphite, a form of carbon, which slows down the fast-moving neutrons that are released each time a uranium atom is split by fission. The moderator helps to keep the fission chain reaction taking place at the best speed for the reactor to work efficiently.

Keeping control

The amount of energy released inside a nuclear reactor is controlled using control rods. These are made of materials such as boron steel, which are strong absorbers of neutrons. The control rods can be lowered and raised between the fuel rods. When they are lowered they absorb neutrons so that fewer uranium atoms undergo fission. If they are lowered completely, the reactor will shut down.

Keeping cool

The heat created by nuclear fission is continually removed from the nuclear reactor. This is done by pumping a coolant through the core of the reactor. The coolant usually flows from the reactor to a structure called a heat exchanger, which transfers heat from one liquid to another, without allowing the liquids to touch. Water in the heat exchanger takes the heat from the coolant and turns into steam, which drives the turbines and produces electricity.

In modern reactors, the coolant is contained in a sealed system, which is closed off from the rest of the reactor. This is to prevent any radioactivity that the coolant might pick up in the reactor from escaping into the surrounding area.

The core (dark circular area) of the Flamanville nuclear reactor in France. The orange crane at the top of the picture carries fuel elements and control rods from a storage area to the reactor's core.

Electricity generated at nuclear power stations is carried away by power lines supported by pylons.

Types of reactor

Spent uranium fuel elements being stored under water in cooling ponds at a reprocessing plant. Later, the fuel rods may be treated to remove the plutonium, which is made into new fuel elements.

There are two main types of nuclear reactors. The most common are thermal reactors. These use natural or slightly enriched uranium as their fuel, and need a moderator to control the fission chain reaction.

Less common are fast reactors. These do not need a moderator to keep the fission chain reaction going steadily.

Fast reactors

Fast reactors use the radioactive element plutonium or a mixture of plutonium and uranium as a fuel. Plutonium is not found naturally in the earth. Instead, it is produced from the poor-quality fuel uranium-238 by reprocessing spent fuel rods from thermal reactors.

Some fast reactors, known as breeders, can make their own fuel. In all fast reactors the fission reaction is controlled so that each fission of an atom produces a number of neutrons. In breeder reactors, these extra neutrons are used to bombard poor-quality fuel materials like uranium-238 and cause them to break up to form better fuels like plutonium-239.

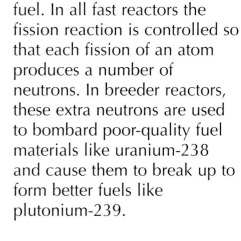

Plutonium for use in fast reactors is produced at reprocessing plants like this one at La Hague in France.

The Superphenix reactor at Creys-Malville in France, the largest fast-breeder reactor in the world.

Advantages and problems

A great advantage of breeder reactors is that they use fuel very efficiently. Under ideal conditions they use almost 100 per cent of the uranium and can produce about 60 times as much energy as a thermal reactor from the same amount of uranium. This helps to save resources; using fast reactors, the world's known supplies of uranium would last for more than 1,000 years.

Breeder reactors have many advantages, but they also have problems. The world's first, and still the largest, breeder reactor, is the Superphenix in France. It began to produce electricity in 1986, but has had to be shut down several times since then because of leaks. Breeder reactors that have been built and tested in the USA, UK, Germany, Russia and Japan have also faced problems such as leaks.

There is a danger that the plutonium used as fuel in breeder reactors could be stolen to make nuclear weapons. Another concern is that breeder reactors can be very expensive to develop.

Many countries have stopped developing breeder reactors. Now, only Japan and France still use them. The Japanese breeder reactor, known as Monju, was shut down at the end of 1995 because of a leak, and repairs were expected to take more than two years.

19

Thermal reactors

Most of the nuclear power plants around the world use thermal reactors. The commonest are the light-water reactors (LWRs). These include both pressurized-water reactors (PWRs) and boiling-water reactors (BWRs).

Over half of the nuclear power reactors used in the world are PWRs. In PWRs, water pumped under high pressure acts as a coolant. This water is prevented from boiling but transfers its heat to water in a separate container, which produces steam.

The BWR is the second most common type of reactor. In a BWR reactor there is no heat exchanger, and water boils in the reactor. Steam coming out from the core is sent directly to a turbine rather than passing through a steam-driven electricity generator.

In countries such as the UK, gas-cooled thermal reactors are more popular. These use a gas, such as carbon dioxide, as a coolant, and graphite as a moderator. Older gas-cooled reactors were called Magnox reactors, after the magnesium alloy used to encase (surround) the uranium fuel. Some Magnox reactors still operate. Later, the UK built advanced gas-cooled reactors (AGRs). These operate at higher temperatures and pressures and produce power more efficiently.

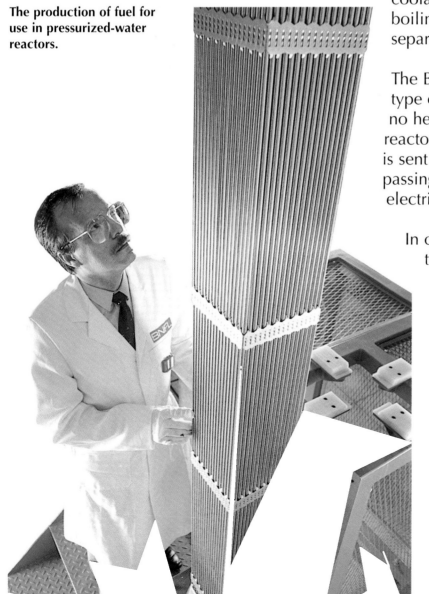

The production of fuel for use in pressurized-water reactors.

Above **A carbon dioxide pump at an advanced gas-cooled reactor at Heysham in the UK. The carbon dioxide gas is pumped through the reactor's core, transferring the heat generated in the core to four boilers, which produce steam.**

Below **The turbines at the Chapelcross Magnox power station in Scotland, UK.**

New designs

Today's gas-cooled reactors are less efficient than PWRs. They also tend to be expensive to build and often suffer from corrosion.

The high-temperature gas-cooled reactor (HTGR), now being tested in Germany and the USA, may solve these problems. It uses helium as the coolant gas and will have a new type of fuel assembly. An advantage of using helium is that it does not cause corrosion. The new fuel assembly means that the system can operate at very high temperatures. This makes it run very efficiently.

New fuel

In India, scientists are working to develop a nuclear reactor which takes advantage of a new fuel source – thorium. Huge amounts of this radioactive element are found in the sand on beaches in India.

Thorium itself cannot be used as a nuclear fuel. However, when it is exposed to neutrons inside a reactor, some of the thorium turns into uranium-233, which can be used as a fuel.

NUCLEAR SAFETY

The Three Mile Island nuclear power plant in Pennsylvania, USA, which was damaged in an accident in 1979.

Many people believe that safety is a major problem with nuclear power. They fear that radioactivity will escape from nuclear power plants and they are not happy with the ways that the nuclear industry disposes of radioactive waste.

Safety measures

The reactor in a nuclear power station contains a large amount of radioactive material within its central core. Properly controlled, this material is not dangerous, but a major accident would release large amounts of radioactivity.

Nuclear plants are strictly controlled by government laws, to try to ensure that radiation will not escape. They are designed so that no uncontrolled radiation can be released, even if the plant is damaged by disasters such as earthquakes, fires or crashing aircraft.

Nuclear reactors are designed to be 'fail-safe'. They automatically shut down if problems occur in the reactor, no matter how these are caused and even if a human operator tries to keep the reactor running. For an accident to occur, a whole chain of failures has to take place.

Accidents happen

Despite safety measures, accidents can still happen. In 1979, an accident damaged the Three Mile Island reactor in the USA. Thanks to the safety systems, only a small amount of radiation was released, but the incident was reported all around the world, and changed many people's attitudes towards nuclear power.

A much more serious accident, which took place in 1986 at the Chernobyl reactor in the Ukraine, changed even more minds (see box). It is said that many more people die each year in road accidents or from breathing in pollution than were affected by the accident at Chernobyl. However, the risk of such terrible destruction has led many people to oppose nuclear power.

Meltdown!

At 1.23 am on Saturday 26 April 1986, operators at the Chernobyl nuclear power station in the Ukraine turned off the automatic safety systems and were carrying out a safety experiment on one of the plant's reactors when things went terribly wrong. The hot fuel element was exposed to water and within a second there was a huge chemical explosion in which the reactor was destroyed. It is estimated that the radioactivity that was released by the accident was 90 times greater than that of the Hiroshima bomb.

Thirty-one people were killed in the explosion and more than 135,000 people had to be evacuated to protect them from the radioactivity. Even so, many people in the area were exposed to the radiation, and no one really knows how this will damage their future health. For example, the radiation may increase the risk that they will develop thyroid cancer. Much smaller amounts of radiation reached other parts of Europe.

The remains of the Chernobyl nuclear power station soon after the accident in April 1986. The accident was caused by a combination of faults in the design and mistakes made by the operators.

Nuclear waste

'The nuclear industry is producing vast amounts of lethal waste, and it doesn't have any idea of what to do with it,' says a representative of the environmental organization Greenpeace. Many people outside the nuclear industry share this view. They think radioactive waste is a dangerous threat to the environment and to people's health.

People who work in the nuclear industry agree that nuclear waste is dangerous, but they argue that it will pose no danger if it is handled properly. They believe they can develop ways of doing this.

Waste disposal

A nuclear power station produces less than 100 m³ of solid radioactive waste each year – just enough to fill up a truck or lorry. The waste is divided into low-, intermediate- and high-level waste, depending on the amount of radioactivity it contains. In Europe and the USA, the nuclear industry aims to dispose of most nuclear waste deep underground, but so far few underground sites have been set up.

A technician using a machine called a Geiger counter to measure radioactivity and to check for leaks of radioactivity from a low-level nuclear waste site in Washington, USA.

Around 95 per cent of the waste from nuclear power stations is low-level waste. Low-level waste includes such things as used protective clothing, air filters and paper towels. Some of it contains no more radioactivity than occurs naturally in Brazil nuts or coffee beans.

Low-level waste only needs a small amount of shielding (protective covering) to make it safe. In the USA, low-level waste is stored at special landfill sites – places where waste is buried in the ground. Elsewhere, most low-level waste is stored above ground in strong waste containers.

Intermediate-level waste from nuclear power stations and fuel reprocessing plants is more radioactive. It includes used reactor parts, equipment that contains traces of radioactivity, and metal fuel cans.

Intermediate-level waste is packaged in cement inside steel drums for disposal. Today it is being stored above ground, but the plan for the future is to build storage sites, or repositories, deep underground.

High-level waste is the most radioactive of all. It consists of the waste from spent fuel which remains after reprocessing has removed the useful uranium and plutonium.

High-level waste is heated to high temperatures and turned into glass blocks. This reduces its volume and makes it safer to store. Eventually, this waste will be buried deep underground. The glass will help to make sure that no radioactivity escapes.
Scientists are also studying other methods of using chemical reactions to break down high-level radioactive waste.

This high-level nuclear waste has been melted by heating to a very high temperature and is being poured into a steel mould where it will cool to form a glass block.

Decommissioning

When a nuclear plant reaches the end of its life it is decommissioned – brought out of service and made safe – by taking away the fuel, burying or removing the reactor and taking apart the buildings.

Fuel transport

Although the fuel for nuclear reactors is not very radioactive, the spent fuel is. To be safe, it must be handled very carefully. After it is removed, spent fuel is placed in deep ponds for several months to allow the radioactivity to die down a little. Afterwards, it is transported to nuclear reprocessing plants or disposal sites. The spent fuel travels in very strong containers, which weigh between 50 and 100 tonnes and have walls more than 30 cm thick. In one test of the containers' strength, scientists drove a 200-tonne train travelling at 160 km per hour into one of these containers. The train was badly damaged, but the container was only scratched.

Above **Nuclear waste being transported through Britain by train. The spent fuel flasks are in the white containers.**

Right **In this British test, a train was crashed into the type of container that would be used to transport spent nuclear fuel, to test its strength.**

The end of production

Several nuclear plants have already been safely
decommissioned, including the Lucens reactor in Switzerland
and a reactor at Shippingport in the USA. In the UK, three
Magnox reactors, Hunterston A and Berkeley in England and
Trawsfynydd in Wales are being dismantled. In France, the
Chinon reactor in the Loire Valley has been turned into a
museum and activity centre to show people how nuclear power
works. It attracts thousands of visitors each year.

Technicians dismantling part of
the Shippingport nuclear reactor
in the USA during the
decommissioning of the plant
in 1982.

NUCLEAR WEAPONS

The city of Hiroshima, Japan, after the dropping of the atomic bomb in 1945. The bomb killed and wounded thousands of people and destroyed buildings over an area of 10 km².

In August 1945 when atomic bombs were dropped on the Japanese cities of Hiroshima and Nagasaki, the USA was the only country to have nuclear weapons. However, after the Second World War, a nuclear arms race began, as other countries worked to develop their own nuclear weapons. By 1949, the Soviet Union had exploded its first atomic bomb. Now France, Britain, China and India also have nuclear weapons and other countries are working to develop them.

The 'big bang'

Nuclear weapons rely on either nuclear fission or fusion to cause explosions. In atomic weapons, energy is released when radioactive elements are split apart by fission. In fusion weapons, also called thermonuclear or hydrogen bombs, the nuclei of hydrogen atoms are squeezed together at very high temperatures until they fuse and form helium nuclei. This releases huge amounts of energy.

President Eisenhower of the USA giving his 'Atoms for Peace' speech at the United Nations General Assembly in 1953.

The force of a nuclear weapon is measured by comparing the number of tonnes of dynamite that it would take to generate as powerful an explosion. Fission bombs give off blasts equivalent to thousands of tonnes of dynamite. Fusion bombs are even more destructive. Their explosions are equivalent to millions of tonnes of dynamite.

Atoms for peace

After the first atomic bombs were developed, President Dwight Eisenhower of the USA took important steps to try to ensure that countries around the world would work together to better understand nuclear power and to use it only for peaceful purposes.

In his 'Atoms for Peace' speech, given to the United Nations (UN) General Assembly in 1953, President Eisenhower proposed setting up an international atomic energy agency to use the power of the atom for the good of all people. The International Atomic Energy Agency (IAEA) was finally set up in 1957. It has 122 member states and reports to the UN General Assembly and to other UN agencies.

The IAEA works to help countries put nuclear energy to peaceful uses and to check that nuclear materials are not used for military purposes. They also support research and training in the use of nuclear energy.

Fission and fusion weapons

A mushroom cloud rises over the Pacific Ocean during a nuclear weapons test. Tests like this are rare because, thanks to nuclear test ban treaties, many countries have agreed to limit the testing of nuclear weapons.

Fission weapons

The atomic bombs dropped on Japan in 1945 were the first fission weapons. Like a nuclear power plant, these weapons use uranium or plutonium as a fuel and rely on a fission chain reaction to release energy. In a nuclear power plant, this chain reaction is carefully controlled. But in an atomic weapon it continues until all the fuel is used up.

A certain amount of fuel, called the critical mass, is needed to start off the chain reaction in an atomic bomb. The size of the critical mass depends on the type and purity of the fuel present. Some weapons use highly enriched uranium as the fuel. Others use plutonium produced in nuclear reactors, such as breeder reactors. An atomic bomb uses at least 10 kg of plutonium or even larger amounts of very highly enriched uranium.

In some atomic weapons, called fission devices, a small piece of fuel is fired down a gun-like barrel so that it hits a second piece of fuel. When the two pieces meet they form a mass greater than the critical mass and the chain reaction starts. In others, known as implosion devices, a hollow ball containing pieces of fuel is surrounded by explosives. When the explosives are set off, they push together the fuel pieces to form a supercritical mass, which starts off the chain reaction.

Fusion weapons

Fusion, or thermonuclear, weapons have the potential to be very much more powerful than atomic weapons. But so far, only very small thermonuclear weapons have been developed.

In fusion bombs, a fission nuclear weapon is used to create the very high temperatures needed to cause the hydrogen atoms to fuse. Inside the bomb, special radiation detectors and reflectors are used to make sure the radiation from the fission weapon travels inwards and presses evenly against a small cylinder, or container, containing the fuel. The radiation starts off the fusion reaction, which in turn, releases huge amounts of energy in a tremendous explosion.

A Pershing missile being fired in Texas, USA. Pershing missiles can carry nuclear warheads and can travel hundreds of kilometres.

Nuclear warheads

The first atomic bombs were so big that they had to be carried by aeroplanes. Now, nuclear weapons can be made very small to fit inside missiles or artillery shells so that they can be launched using large guns. These small weapons are called warheads. Some nuclear warheads are fitted to long-range (strategic) nuclear weapons, which are designed to attack targets a long way away. They may also be fitted to shorter-range (tactical) weapons, for use over shorter distances in the battlefield.

Destructive power

The explosion from a nuclear weapon causes huge amounts of damage. But that is only the beginning of the destruction. The bombs give off a blinding light and burning heat. Temperatures can reach millions of degrees centigrade. The tremendous heat is absorbed by the surrounding air and creates a fireball that can be seen hundreds of kilometres away.

Nuclear bombs also give off deadly radiation. The radiation makes elements in the surrounding area radioactive, and these radioactive elements, known as fallout, can remain in the environment for hundreds of years and can be carried over great distances by the wind.

This US Navy submarine is carrying long-range, strategic nuclear warheads, designed to deter foreign powers from attacking the USA.

A demonstration against nuclear weapons in London, UK, in 1961. The first anti-nuclear organizations were set up in the 1950s and, since then, there have been organized anti-nuclear protests worldwide.

The nuclear threat

Many scientists believe that a nuclear attack could lead to a change in the weather because the burning of cities and forests would send smoke into the atmosphere, blacking out heat from the Sun. This could lead to a 'nuclear winter' with low temperatures that might last for months. The effects of nuclear explosions could also damage the ozone layer, a layer of gas which protects the Earth from ultraviolet rays from the Sun.

Fortunately, this grim prospect has been enough to deter governments from using the nuclear weapons that they have built. So far, the atomic bombs dropped on Hiroshima and Nagasaki are the only nuclear weapons that have ever been used in war. But the nuclear arms race continues because many countries believe that having nuclear weapons will discourage others from attacking them.

President Reagan of the USA and President Gorbachov of the USSR embrace at the Moscow Summit in 1988 after agreeing to limit the development of nuclear weapons.

POWER FOR GOOD

After the first atomic bomb was tested, Enrico Fermi wrote that he would be very surprised if the knowledge gained during the project did not lead to 'an outcome more spectacular' for peaceful purposes. His prediction turned out to be correct.

The idea of using radioactive materials frightens many people but, when used properly, radioactivity can save lives and help industry to work more efficiently.

Information from isotopes

Nuclear reactors can be used to produce radioactive isotopes. These isotopes provide a useful way of looking inside things. Because they can be easily spotted using radiation detectors, the isotopes can be used as 'tracers'. The isotopes are fed into a system along with other materials and a radiation detector is used to show where the materials go.

Radioactive tracers have many uses. For example, geologists use them to follow the flow of water through underground systems.

A woman receiving a gamma scan of her lungs. The radiation is introduced into the body by injection or by being swallowed and it shows up on the screen.

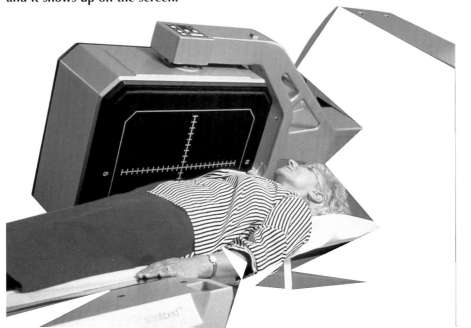

Doctors can use radioactive tracers to find out what is wrong with patients. The tracers can be safely swallowed by patients and their journey through the body photographed using a special camera. The tracers help doctors to see how organs such as the heart, liver, thyroid gland and brain are working without the patient having to undergo an operation.

Cleaning up

Because it kills harmful organisms, radiation is a useful way of sterilizing food and medical supplies. In some countries, radiation may be used instead of chemicals to preserve food and prevent the spread of diseases carried on food.

When food is irradiated, it is exposed to radiation. This kills insects, bacteria and other organisms that might spoil the food or cause diseases. The food does not become radioactive. Food irradiation has many advantages. It takes less energy to irradiate food than it would to keep it cold in refrigerators. Also, irradiation does not leave any traces of chemicals behind, something that often happens when chemicals are used to preserve food. However, food irradiation is controversial and some people believe that further research into its long term effects is required.

A technician in California, USA, irradiating a container of fruit. The irradiation is carried out under water to protect technicians from radiation.

Saving lives with radiation

In hospitals, radiation can be a lifesaver, helping doctors to examine their patients so that they can diagnose and cure diseases. If you have ever had an X-ray at a hospital or at the dentist's you have already experienced one of the commonest ways that radiation is used to help doctors create images so that they can 'see' inside the human body.

Positron emission tomography (PET)

PET (positron emission tomography) scanners are devices which scan and examine a patient's body. They provide doctors with a clearer view of the heart and brain than an X-ray. Before a patient is scanned, they are given an injection of a radioactive tracer into their bloodstream. The scanner carries out a series of scans of the patient's body to detect where the radiation has travelled. This information is processed by a computer to give very detailed pictures of the inside of the patient.

A woman about to undergo radiotherapy for a brain tumour. Radiation kills cancer cells and radiotherapy can cure some types of cancer.

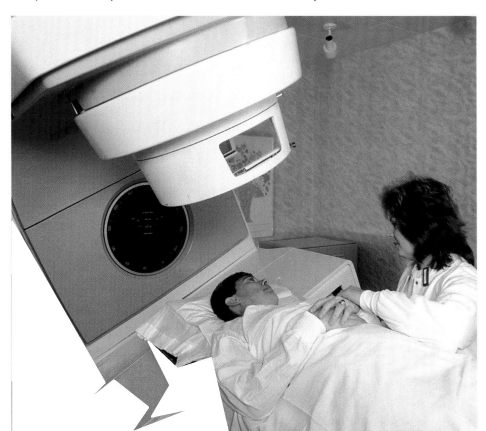

Containers full of medical equipment being positioned over a source of gamma irradiation. The irradiation will sterilize the equipment.

Radiotherapy

For many cancer patients, radiation can be a valuable treatment because it kills cancer cells. Some forms of cancer can be cured using radiation and others are slowed down or the pain reduced. Doctors use computers to focus high levels of radiation on the cancer cells to kill them. The treatment can make patients feel ill for a time afterwards, but many feel this is a small price to pay for getting rid of the cancer. Other types of cancer can be treated by putting a small radioactive pellet or 'seed' inside the body near the cancer cells to kill them.

Keeping clean

Radiation is also a good way of sterilizing equipment and supplies in hospitals. Because the radiation can pass through many materials, equipment can be sealed in plastic while it is sterilized. It can then be left sealed in the plastic to keep it clean until it is needed.

Exploring our environment

Radioactivity can help scientists study our world. Under the sea or out in space, where it can be difficult to take on fuel, nuclear power can be the answer. It provides a compact energy source for vehicles such as submarines, cruisers, aircraft carriers and spacecraft that must travel long distances without taking on more fuel.

At sea

Nuclear submarines rely on small nuclear reactors for their power. Normal submarines have to come up to the surface regularly to run their engines in air and take on new fuel. Nuclear submarines do not have to do this, which means they can stay under water for very long periods of time.

The first nuclear submarine, *Nautilus*, was built in the USA in 1955. It was the first submarine to cross the Arctic below the ice-cap. Now, Britain, France and Russia have also developed nuclear submarines.

Out in space

Nuclear reactors are a useful way to generate power in outer space, especially for long missions where it is difficult to refuel. The *Apollo 12* Moon mission in 1969 is just one of the many US and Russian spacecraft that have relied on nuclear power. Scientists believe nuclear power will be even more important in future missions as they attempt to explore further into space.

One of the astronauts on the *Apollo 12* mission removes a fuel element from its cask.

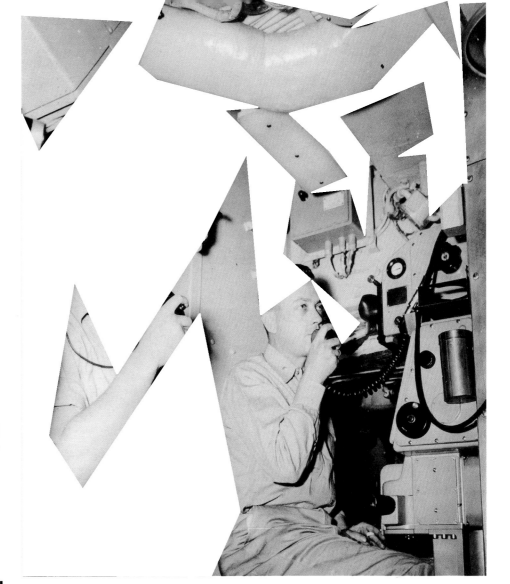

US navy personnel aboard the *Nautilus*, the world's first nuclear-powered submarine, during its underwater trip across the Atlantic from the UK to New York, USA.

On the sea surface, nuclear power is used on some warships and ice-breakers. Nuclear reactors were tested on cargo ships, too, but they turned out to be expensive, and many people had safety fears and did not want these nuclear-powered ships to land in their ports.

Exploring underground

Geologists looking for oil and gas rely on measurements of radioactivity to help them discover what kinds of rocks and liquids lie below the Earth's surface. When they drill wells, they usually record information about them, using special tools called sensors to get information about what lies below ground. Several of these tools rely on radiation.

The gamma-ray tool records the natural radiation given off by rocks. This gives important information about the type of rock and the minerals in it. Other tools contain their own radioactive sources and detectors. They send out neutrons into the surrounding rock and the radiation detector records how the rocks are affected by the radiation. Geologists study this information to help them understand more about the rocks and whether they contain oil, gas or water in the tiny spaces between the grains of rock.

A DIFFICULT DECISION

Whatever the future holds, we know that the world's energy needs will probably continue to grow. How will we solve the energy problem? The choice is difficult.

Around two-thirds of the electricity generated today is produced in power plants that burn fossil fuels. But these fuels will not last for ever, and once they are used up, they cannot be replaced. Burning fossil fuels also releases sulphur dioxide – a cause of acid rain – and carbon dioxide, an important contributor to the greenhouse effect. The US Environmental Protection Agency estimates that about 60–65 per cent of greenhouse gases generated as a result of human activity are produced directly or indirectly by energy use.

What about renewable sources?

More than 20 per cent of the world's electricity needs are generated using renewable energy sources such as energy from rivers, tides, the wind, the Sun or heat from below the Earth's surface. These sources will never run out and they cause far less pollution.

A forest in the Czech Republic showing the effects of acid rain. Acid rain has killed many trees in parts of central Europe.

The Benmore hydroelectric dam in New Zealand. Renewable energy sources like hydroelectricity have many advantages but also have some environmental drawbacks.

Renewable energy sources do have some disadvantages. It is more expensive to produce electricity this way. In addition, it is currently not possible to meet the huge energy needs of large industrialized nations using renewable sources alone.

Hydroelectric plants, which use energy from fast-flowing rivers, already provide around one-sixth of the world's energy supplies. But they too have some drawbacks. Suitable rivers are not available everywhere. And some giant hydroelectric schemes have caused environmental problems because they destroy landscapes and animal habitats.

Nuclear power

Nuclear power plants give off few of the gases associated with acid rain and the greenhouse effect, and replacing coal-fired power stations with nuclear power plants helps to reduce the amount of carbon dioxide given off. Nuclear power also helps to conserve (save) fossil fuels for other uses. For example, oil is needed to make plastics and petrol.

However, many people are very worried about the safety of nuclear plants. And no one has yet found a completely safe way of disposing of nuclear waste forever. There are other worries too. Plutonium, the fuel used in fast reactors and produced in breeder reactors, is also used to make nuclear bombs. Could nuclear reactor technology help more countries develop nuclear weapons of their own?

A question of balance

Who is right? The scientists and engineers working in the nuclear industry who believe that it will be possible to solve all the safety and waste disposal problems? Or the anti-nuclear protesters, who believe that nuclear power can damage the environment and people's health; lead to more nuclear weapons, and is not needed anyway?

There is no perfect energy source. Each has advantages and disadvantages, so it is very important for countries to consider their energy needs carefully and develop balanced energy programmes that do not rely heavily on just one energy source, or ignore other sources completely.

Fusion for the future

Some scientists believe that using nuclear fusion to generate electricity could solve our future energy needs without damaging the environment and without the risk of nuclear accidents.

In the fusion reaction, two isotopes of hydrogen, deuterium and tritium, are heated to millions of degrees to force them to fuse to form helium and release neutrons. These are captured in a surrounding blanket of lithium, the lightest metal. Heat from this reaction can be used to drive an electricity generator.

The Savannah River tritium facility, USA. Tritium, an isotope of hydrogen, is an important fuel for fusion power research. It is also used in thermonuclear, or fusion, atomic bombs.

The fuels needed for fusion are plentiful and easy to find. Deuterium is found wherever there is water. Lithium exists in many rocks. Tritium does not exist naturally, but it can be produced in a fusion reactor by bombarding lithium with neutrons. Nuclear fusion plants should be safe because any malfunction would cause them to shut down. Also, the radioactive water they produce has a relatively short half-life.

The problem

But there is just one problem. No one has yet succeeded in building a working fusion reactor.

Fusion research is being carried out in several countries, including the USA, Japan and Russia. The biggest and most successful fusion research project in the world is the Joint European Torus (JET) programme, based in Culham, UK.

The JET nuclear fusion experiment at Culham, UK.

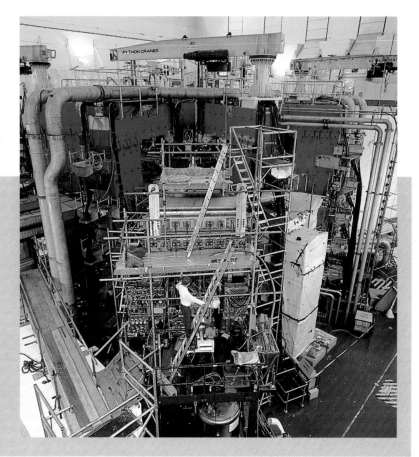

The JET programme

The JET programme began in 1978 and now nearly 400 scientists and engineers from 16 European countries are working on the project. There is still much to do, but the JET team is confident of success. They hope to set up a full-scale fusion power plant by the year 2030. By the end of the twenty-first century, they predict that fusion will supply as much of the world's electricity needs as fossil fuels do today.

DATE CHART

1789 Martin Kalproth discovers uranium.

1895 Wilhelm Röntgen discovers X-rays.

1896 Henri Becquerel discovers radioactivity.

1897 Joseph John Thompson identifies the electron.

1913 Niels Bohr introduces his model for the radioactive atom.

1919 Ernest Rutherford becomes the first person to split the atom.

1932 James Chadwick discovers the neutron.

1934 Enrico Fermi bombards uranium with neutrons.

1939 Scientists in the USA, Denmark and France independently confirm the phenomenon of nuclear fission.

1942 Enrico Fermi demonstrates the world's first nuclear reactor in Chicago, USA on 2 December.

1945 The first atomic bomb is tested in New Mexico, USA.
The first atomic bomb is dropped on Hiroshima, Japan, followed by a second atomic bomb, dropped on Nagasaki, Japan.

1946 The Atomic Energy Research Establishment is set up at Harwell, UK.

1947 The first nuclear reactor in Western Europe (GLEEP, or Graphite Low Energy Experimental Pile) is constructed at Harwell, UK.

1953 President Dwight Eisenhower of the USA makes his 'Atoms for Peace' speech at the United Nations General Assembly.

1956 The world's first commercial nuclear power plant commissioned at Calder Hall, Cumbria in the UK.

1957 The first large nuclear accident takes place with a fire and radiation leak at the Windscale reactor in the UK.
The International Atomic Energy Agency is set up by the United Nations.

1970 The nuclear non-proliferation treaty comes into force.

1978 The Joint European Torus (JET) fusion project begins at Culham, UK.

1979 Accident at the Three Mile Island nuclear power station in the USA.

1985 The reactor at Three Mile Island is restarted.

1986 A meltdown occurs at the Chernobyl nuclear reactor in the Ukraine.

1995 Despite protests from around the world, French scientists carry out underground nuclear test explosions in the South Pacific.

GLOSSARY

absorbers Materials that soak up substances.

acid rain Rain that is more acid than normal and can damage plants, animals, metal and buildings. It is produced when gases produced by pollution react with rain-water.

alloy A mixture of two or more metals.

arms race The race between different countries to build more nuclear weapons than other nations.

artillery shells Missiles fired from large, heavy guns used for fighting on land.

atomic bombs Bombs dropped from the air that use the release of nuclear energy to cause large explosions.

biomass fuels Fuels like wood, crop waste and animal dung, which are made up of material produced by recently living plants and animals.

bombarded Threw lots of objects at.

boron steel A type of steel that contains the element boron.

chain reaction A series of events, each one caused by the one before.

concentrated Made stronger.

coolant A material that removes heat to help control the temperature.

corrosion A chemical reaction that weakens metal.

crystalline Made from crystals.

diagnose To identify a disease.

environment The chemical, physical and biological conditions that exist on Earth.

evacuated Moved from an area because of danger.

fission The process of splitting apart the nucleus of an atom, releasing energy and particles.

fossil fuels Natural fuels which are extracted from the ground, like coal and oil.

geologists Scientists who study the Earth and its rocks.

greenhouse effect The way in which the Sun's heat is trapped around the Earth by gases which have built up in the Earth's atmosphere and prevent the heat from escaping.

greenhouse gases Gases which contribute to the greenhouse effect.

habitats The places in which plants and animals live.

malfunction When something does not work at all or does not work properly.

mass Amount of matter.

meltdown A situation that occurs when the fission reaction gets out of control. The heat produced can cause the core of a nuclear reactor to melt.

missiles Weapons that travel under their own power, sometimes for very long distances.

neutrons Particles in the nuclei of atoms that carry a neutral (neither positive nor negative) electrical charge.

nuclear reactor A power station where energy is produced as a result of a nuclear reaction.

ore A rock from which useful substances can be obtained.

particles Tiny pieces.

photographic plate A light-sensitive glass that was used to record images before photographic film was available.

radiation detectors Machines, such as Geiger counters, that find and measure radioactivity.

radioactive Isotopes, the nuclei of which break down giving off energy and atomic particles.

rays Narrow beams of particles, light or other forms of energy.

self-sustaining A reaction that keeps going without any

outside force.
sterilizing Cleaning, by killing germs and bacteria.
supercritical mass An amount greater than the critical mass.
turbine A machine that is driven by a flow of steam, gas or water.
ultraviolet rays A type of electromagnetic radiation or wave.
X-ray A type of electromagnetic radiation or wave which can travel through objects that light cannot penetrate.

FIND OUT MORE

Books to read

Inside a Nuclear Power Plant by Charlotte Wilcox (Carolrhoda Books, 1995)
Chernobyl: The Ongoing Story of the World's Deadliest Nuclear Disaster by Glenn Cheney
   (New Discovery Books, 1994)
Nuclear Energy – Nuclear Waste by Anne Glaperin (Chelsea House Publishers, 1992)
Nuclear Power by Nigel Hawkes (Wayland, 1989)

Write to:

British Nuclear Industry Forum (BNIF), 22 Buckingham Gate, London SW1E 6LR.
AEA Technology, 329 Harwell, Didcot, Oxon. OX11, 0RA.
Culham Laboratory, Abingdon, Oxon. OX14 3DB, UK (for information about JET).
CND, 162 Holloway Road, London N7 8DQ.

Places to visit

AEA Technology, Dounreay, Thurso, Caithness KW14 7TZ.
Sellafield Visitors Centre, British Nuclear Fuels Plc, Seascale, Cumbria CA20 1PG.
Calder Hall Power Station, Sellafield Visitors Centre (address as above).
Sizewell Visitor Centre, Nuclear Electric Plc, Sizewell, Leiston, Suffolk IP16 4UR.
Dungeness Information Centre, Nuclear Electric Plc, Romney Marsh, Kent TN29 9PP.
Wylfa Power Station, Nuclear Electric Plc, Cemaes Bay, Anglesey, Gwynedd LL67 0DH.
Hinkley Point A and B Power Stations, Nuclear Electric Plc, Bridgewater, Somerset, TA5 1UD.

INDEX